If It Had Not Been for God!

CYNTHIA B. MAISONET

PAGE PUBLISHING, INC.
New York, NY

First originally published by Page Publishing, Inc. 2014

ISBN 978-1-63417-359-9 (pbk)
ISBN 978-1-63417-360-5 (digital)

Printed in the United States of America

To my children, Devin, Diedra, and Leelee who
inspired me and encouraged me every step of the way. I
love you.

Isaiah 53:5

But He was wounded for our transgressions, He was
bruised for our iniquities, the chastisement for our peace
was upon Him, and by His stripes we are healed.

A Godly Reflection

Psalm 46:1, "God is our refuge and strength,
a very present help in trouble."

This scripture lets us know that God is looking out for us, He has our back. When we are facing trouble, God is there to rescue us. Take a moment and think back to certain situations and think about how you were able to get past them. It was nobody but God who rescued you, and now you can look back on that time as a life experience. Just take some time and think back and know that had it not been for God on your side, where would you be?

Introduction

This is a story about a little girl named Mercy, who against all odds and by the world's standards should have become a statistic of society. By God's love and His amazing saving grace Mercy was able to be rescued out of the devil's grip and live a normal and productive life. This story proves that when God is in your life there is nothing or no one who can stop you. We all face obstacles and stumbling blocks in our life, but through God, He can and will give your life meaning if you let Him.

I

No Fun and Games

Mercy, who was the youngest of three children, was introduced to abuse at an early age. The first form of abuse that Mercy was introduced to was sexual abuse. She was introduced to this form of abuse by her grandfather. Mercy's grandfather was a very mean-spirited man. He saw the children as a burden to him and his wife. Grandpa, as he was known by the children, had his own ideas on how he could get some gratification out of this current situation of being the children's guardian. Grandpa would keep the girls in the house, saying that they needed to do chores. Mercy's brother was allowed to go outside. While in the house, Mercy and her sister Grace would clean the house spotless. After the girls were finished, Grandpa would call Grace to him. He would then ask her if she wanted to go outside. Grace would answer yes, and Grandpa would then take her in his room and do things to her. They would be in his room for what seemed like forever to Mercy. However, when Grace came out, the girls would be allowed to go outside. Being that Mercy was very young at the time, Grace would tell her that Grandpa just wanted to play a game.

In order to protect Mercy, Grace would play the game with Grandpa for the both of them. Sometimes Mercy would sit in the living room to keep watch and make sure no one was coming while Grace and Grandpa played the game. Mercy was curious to know what the game was and why they always had to go in the room to play. Grace promised to tell Mercy about the game when she was a little older, but what Grace didn't know was even though Grandpa played with her he also played with Mercy. There were times when Mercy was in the house alone with Grandpa, and it was during these times that Grandpa had his way with her. When he finished, he would give Mercy a dollar and tell her not to tell, for if she did she would be severely punished. Grace and Mercy endured this treatment and never told anyone what was being done to them by their grandfather. On the outside, the sisters appeared to be happy children, but on the inside they were both carrying a painful secret. The children's grandmother, whom they called Nanny, took a small side job to help with household expenses because she and her husband were on a fixed income. Mercy's brother Joseph Jr., who loved sports, stayed out of the house as much as possible because he didn't like the living conditions.

Although the family did not have a lot of money, Nanny did the best that she could for her grandchildren. She did the best that she could to keep the apartment neat and clean despite her painful arthritis. Nanny was quite relieved to have help from her granddaughters Grace and Mercy. Joseph Jr. hated that they couldn't have nice things like the other neighborhood children. He also was angry that he had to live with his grandparents instead of his mom and dad. Staying outside helped him deal with the inside a little better. Waking up not knowing what the next day would bring into their lives was very scary to the children. Mercy wasn't aware that the game that Grandpa played with her and Grace was wrong, but she dared not say a word for fear of the punishment that Grandpa threatened her with. One thing that Mercy was blessed with was a very unique imagination. To escape the pain and fear that was happening to her, whenever Mercy watched TV she would imagine that she was one of the characters on the show. Everyone was happy and loved. No one was hurting, in pain, or even sad; at least in Mercy's eyes. Mercy thought that everything was perfect on TV. Whatever was wrong usually ended up being made better by the end of the show. Mercy wondered if this type of life really existed where people were kind to one another and genuinely cared for each other.

Mercy's grandparents would go out and visit with their family in another part of New Jersey. They would take the children along with them and stay for the weekend. Mercy loved these visits very much. It gave Mercy a time to get away, and it also helped her to see how other people interacted with their families. The family that she loved visiting the most was that of Grandpa's brother and his wife. They lived in a trailer home, but when you went inside it looked like a regular house. Mercy thought that they had to be rich to have such a nice house and two cars. Grandpa didn't even own one. Mercy and her siblings were very much loved by their aunt Lula and their uncle Foreman. While there they would take them to the store and buy all sorts of treats for them. Mercy loved this treatment that she received while away. She absorbed it like a sponge, because she knew that it would eventually come to an end. She would always find someone to play with while there. The country life seemed to be nice and easygoing. Mercy thought to herself when she got older she would love to live in the country. There was always food being cooked outside on the grill, and the grown folks would always be laughing and talking over old times. Mercy found some of the stories to be so interesting. They would also drink and carry on before it got late and it was time for everyone to turn in for the night. To Mercy this was the good life. No worries, or at least she thought.

While visiting Aunt Lula and Uncle Foreman, the kids were treated like royalty. Whenever Grandpa tried to chastise them in any way, Aunt Lula would step in and tell Grandpa to leave the children alone. Aunt Lula would make sure that the children had a good time and that they behaved themselves while visiting. No harsh words were ever used toward the children. They received nothing but love and kindness while visiting. Sometimes their other grandchildren came down to visit while Mercy and her siblings were there. Having so much family and friends around made life that much sweeter. Mercy knew that family was important, and she welcomed all of the love and attention that she received while being away from home. Mercy would constantly think about what was going to transpire once she returned home. Mercy was also curious to know whether her cousins played any games like the one that Grandpa played with her and her sister. It remained a question in the back of her mind only, for she was afraid to ask anyone or tell anyone what she and her sister were being made to do. For the time being, she continued to think happy thoughts and pretend that she could stay in this place forever. As life would have it, all good times must come to an end. It was time to return to the city. Mercy cried when it was time to leave her aunt and uncle. Mercy and her siblings were invited to visit as much as they wanted. Mercy didn't want to just visit, she wanted to stay.

Chapter 1

MINISTRY MOMENT

Even as little children we go through trials and tribulations, but just know that we are not alone. In Jeremiah 1:5, the Bible says: "Before I formed you in the womb I knew (and) approved of you (as My chosen instrument), and before you were born I separated and set you apart, consecrating you; (and) I appointed you as a prophet to the nations."

God knows us all. He knows that there are going to be things that we are going to have to experience in our lives, but He is there with us to bring us through. Being a prophet unto the nations just means that we have to share our story with the world. No one has the same testimony, but it is our job to give someone else hope through our individual stories. The world needs to see God at work in your life. If you are reading this book, it only means that God has brought you through and now you have a job to do. Give God glory for all that He has done in your life and share Him with others who may be feeling helpless and hopeless. Just know that you are still here for a reason. So don't waste another minute in despair and defeat. Get up and tell someone about God's healing power today.

II

Only the Love that My Mother Could Give

There were times when Mercy's mother came to visit the children. It seemed as though whenever the children saw her she would always be in a hurry because there was always someone waiting for her. Dorothy or Dot, as she was known, usually came around when she was intoxicated. The children were always happy to see her and would beg her to stay, but as time would have it she would always be on her way to her next alcoholic adventure. When Dorothy came around she would have stories for days about how she went here and there and had such a good time. Never once did she mention that she missed her children. One thing was definitely sure, you couldn't hold Momma down. She couldn't stay still long enough to create some sort of stability in her life. To her, life was just one great big party. She was in constant search of that next quick good time. Dorothy would always be on a trip to God knows where, with God knows who. She always made her life seem so great and grand to everyone she knew. But was it really? Only time would tell.

One day, as Mercy was walking down one of the blocks in the neighborhood, she came upon her mother in a drunken, disheveled mess, sitting on some stairs in a hallway. It hurt Mercy to see her mother in this condition. Mercy went over to her mother, calling and nudging her until she gave an answer. Dorothy was so intoxicated that she couldn't remember how she got there or how long she had been there. Mercy thought that if her mom was to come and live with her and her siblings everything would get better for her. Mercy thought that if this were to happen, then she wouldn't have to worry about finding her mom in someone's hallway or someplace worse. The thing that Mercy didn't realize was that her mother had an illness: she was an alcoholic. Dorothy was in the grips of her disease and couldn't help herself or her children. There were nights when Mercy couldn't sleep for fear that her mother was out there somewhere in an alley, or worse, alone and crying for help. This was just another secret burden that Mercy carried around with her. Mercy's life went on like this for quite some time until what she thought was a ray of hope came to the rescue of her and her siblings.

Mercy's father came to take the children with him to Kentucky where he was stationed. Not aware of what had been taking place while he was away, he seemed happy to see his mother and the children. Joseph Sr. stayed in town for a little while, visiting old friends and catching up on old times. He even got the opportunity to be reacquainted with his father, whom he hadn't seen since he was a teen-ager. Now that all of his visiting was out of the way, he thanked his mother and her husband for taking care of the children while he was away. Mercy was happy and sad at the same time; happy for a better life, and sad because she would have to leave her grandmother. Mercy was also upset that she didn't get a chance to say goodbye to her mother. Joseph packed the children up and headed back to Kentucky. While on the road, all Mercy could think about was her mom and that she could be somewhere yelling for help and there was nothing that she or anyone else could do to save her. This ride seemed like it would never end only because of all of the fear that was on the inside of Mercy. Mercy also wondered if she would have to play the same games with her father that she played with Grandpa. Mercy closed her eyes and began to think happy thoughts.

While Mercy's eyes were closed, she imagined that she was in a field of pretty flowers and she and her siblings were happy and playing together. She imagined that everyone was happy and there was love being shown everywhere. Her mother was there and she wasn't intoxicated. She was smiling and very clean and pretty. Her dad was there, holding hands with her mom, and both of them were laughing and having a wonderful time. Mercy kept her eyes shut, for she knew that when she opened them all of the happiness would be taken away by fear and sadness over her current living situation. While her eyes were closed, she even imagined that her family was rich and had a lot of very nice things. They even had a dog. All of these beautiful visions kept a smile on Mercy's face. She was hoping and praying for at least a little bit of happiness when they reached their destination. Was it so far-fetched to hope for her parents to reconcile? Maybe that's what her mom needed. Well, Mercy had a very hopeful heart. Finally it was time to leave the happy place and contend with reality. Their journey was over. They had arrived at their new home. From the looks of things, maybe there was something to having a hopeful heart. Mercy began to smile to herself. "Let's just see how this is going to play out." And with that, they were unpacking the car and stepping into a new home and new beginning with their father.

Chapter 2

MINISTRY MOMENT

Sometimes we go through things and the only way to escape the pain of the situation is for us to create pleasant thoughts in our mind. The Bible tells us in II Timothy 1:7, "For God has not given us a spirit of fear, but of power and of love and of a sound mind."

It is okay to use your imagination to think good things. Your mind is also the place where you see things before they happen, such as your healing from all of the guilt, hurt, and shame of your past. If you can believe it, with God's help you can achieve it.

III

Father Knows Best

Living with their father seemed to be a breath of fresh air compared to the life that they had with their grandparents. The house was huge. There was an upstairs, with two bathrooms, and each one of the children had their own room. Mercy loved this. It really felt like home to her even in her heart. The refrigerator was always full, and there was a double-door freezer also full of food. There were all kinds of goodies in the pantry and in the cabinets. There was a washing machine and dryer. Man, oh man, thought Mercy. She was so excited. All she could do was skip everywhere she went. There was a bike for each of them also. Mercy couldn't believe her eyes when she saw her bike. She couldn't wait to go outside and ride it either. Mercy thought she couldn't be any happier than she was at this time in her life. She was at her own house, not someone else's house and pretending that it was hers. It really was hers. Their father had a dog. The dog was beautiful. Mercy had all new clothes, so many new outfits to choose from. Now Mercy could actually be a child and do all of the things that a child could do without any special games or secrets. This was the best. Although she wondered about her mom from time to time, Mercy couldn't be happier. No one was going to hurt her or her sister ever again, or so she thought. Since it was still summer, Mercy got a chance to go outside and get used to her new surroundings. The neighborhood children seemed nice. Everyone seemed happy, at least to Mercy. This new life was definitely a dream come true for Mercy and her siblings. Well, soon school would be starting. Mercy was even excited to go to school. She was excited about meeting new friends and learning new things. Well, goodbye, summer, and hello, fall, a season of new beginnings.

Mercy started her new school with much anticipation. The teachers were very nice. Even her classmates seemed very nice. Mercy made a lot of new friends. After school Mercy did her homework, and after that she did what she loved to do most: she went outside and played until her father came home from work. When Mercy's father came home, Mercy would greet him with a great big hug and kiss because she was glad to see him. Whenever her father was at home, Mercy felt safe and loved the same way she should have felt when she was living with her grandparents. It wasn't too long after the children arrived that their father began dating. He would go out with different women a couple of times per week. He seemed to be enjoying himself. As long as he was happy, the children were happy for him. No one or nothing would ever take the place of his children in his life. Joseph Sr. enjoyed spending family time with them. Sometimes he would take them out for dinner, to the movies, shopping, or order pizza and watch movies at home. Whatever they did, they did it together as a family. Joseph began to grow tired of the dating scene and expressed a desire to settle down. Not too soon after the fact, Joseph Sr. found someone whom he became very fond of. Although they dated for only a short time, Joseph Sr. decided to marry this woman. There was no elaborate ceremony or celebration of any sort, which was very strange to the children. The only thing that the children knew was that this was their father's wife. Joseph Sr.'s wife, Karen, seemed to be nice. She had a beautiful little girl from a previous relationship. The baby's name was Crystal and she was still an infant. Now the Carters were one big happy family thrown together from different walks of life.

The children's happiness was very short-lived once their father returned home from his honeymoon. Not too long after their return, the rules of the house seemed to change. It seemed as though Mercy's dad had been hypnotized, or better yet, brainwashed while he was away from the children. Joseph Sr. no longer had a mind of his own; instead, he went along with everything that his new wife wanted or said. Joseph Sr. became a stranger to his children. Mercy couldn't understand what had happened to bring about such a drastic change. Mercy didn't know who her dad was anymore. All of the love and attention that the children received from their father came to an end also. Mercy thought, "How could my dad change overnight?" Now, instead of talking to his children, all they heard were orders being given. Now there were orders with punishments included. What was once a happy home was now being turned into an army boot camp. Gone were the happy times that Mercy and her dad shared. Gone was the quality time that Joseph Sr. spent with his children at home. Gone were all the things that the Carter children came to know and love from being with their father—all at the hands of one woman, Mrs. Karen Carter. It seemed as though she couldn't wait to get in and get started manipulating everything in the house. The children didn't like their stepmother at all.

Karen was the type of woman who was very cunning and dominating when it came to Joseph Sr.'s relationship with his children. Karen would suggest things and Joseph Sr. would go along with the suggestions that were made. If what she proposed wasn't carried out to her standards, then a punishment would be handed out. Pretty soon the girls felt more like maids than children. Even the food that the children had come to know and love turned into food that Karen liked only. Karen didn't cook very often. She preferred to eat out instead. Karen and Joseph Sr. began dining out quite frequently. When Karen and Joseph Sr. dined out, the children remained at home, usually having to fend for themselves when it came to dinner. While their father and his new wife dined out lavishly, all the children had to look forward to was a double-door freezer full of pot pies. There was no more going out to eat with Dad. Gone were the happy times that the children shared with their father before Karen came into their lives. Being that Grace was older than Mercy, she rebelled against this unfair treatment and left her father's house.

Chapter 3

MINISTRY MOMENT

Ephesians 6:1 NLT, "Children, obey your parents because you belong to the Lord, for this is the right thing to do."

We do not choose our parents. God knows all things, so therefore He knows what's going to take place in our lives before we do. All we have to do is obey them and be the best children we can be no matter what happens. If you are constantly putting your best foot forward when it comes to your parents, then you are honoring God. When God sees your obedience, He will then move on your behalf in one way or another. Everything in life happens for a reason. If you are facing difficulties at the hands of your parents, pray and continue on in what you are doing, always putting your best foot forward, and let God bless you for your efforts.

IV

Duty Calls

The list of chores for Mercy just kept growing. Another chore that Mercy had the pleasure of executing was diaper duty. Karen only used cloth diapers for the baby, and when they became soiled, she would soak the soiled diaper in the toilet. It was Mercy's job to scrub the soiled diaper by hand before putting it into the washing machine. This chore would have to be done all day, every day. Even while Mercy was in school, there would be soiled diapers soaking in the toilet when she came home. No more going outside after she finished her homework. Now it was just chores, chores, and more chores. No more excitement when her father came home from work. Now there was only fear and sadness; the fear of being punished for the least little thing, and sadness because now she was feeling unloved once again. It seemed as though Joseph Sr. came home looking for a reason to punish Mercy. Now, every time her father's car pulled up she would become nervous and a knot of fear would form in the pit of her stomach. "What is going on? Why am I afraid of my own father?" Mercy just couldn't understand.

One day after school, one of Mercy's classmates knocked on her door and asked to speak to someone. Karen came to the door. After the child left, Karen called Mercy upstairs to the bathroom. While in the bathroom, Karen made Mercy eat an entire bar of bath soap. After she was finished, Mercy was then made to drink a cup of dish detergent after it. After this was finished, Karen looked at Mercy and said, "Now hopefully this will help to keep your mouth clean." Mercy couldn't understand why this was happening. Mercy asked her stepmother what she meant by the statement that was just made. Mercy's classmate said that Mercy had cussed at school during recess. Mercy had completely forgotten about what had taken place at school. Karen couldn't wait to tell Mercy's dad about what Mercy's classmate had said. Now, to add insult to injury, Mercy was also beaten and punished when her father came home. Not only was Mercy sick from the soap and dish detergent, but she was also hurt from the beating that she received from her father. The most hurtful part about the whole situation was the fact that Mercy never got a chance to tell her side of the story.

Mercy would cry herself to sleep at night because she couldn't understand why this was happening. Gone was the care that Mercy received from her father. Mercy felt like she was in a cruel world all alone, with no one to talk to for fear that no one would listen. Mercy was also afraid that word would get back to her father and she would be punished for telling. What happened to all of the love, attention, and affection from her father? It was as though the rug had been pulled out from underneath her feet. Mercy couldn't wait to grow up. The first chance that she got, she was getting out on her own. Mercy said to herself, "When I grow up and have children I am going to love them forever. I am going to listen to them. I am never going to beat or mistreat them." In essence, she would treat them the opposite of how she was being treated. Whenever she could, Mercy would go into her room and think about how things used to be for her and her family. She missed those times dearly. Mercy thought that if she stayed out of sight she couldn't get in trouble. Contrary to what Mercy thought, things just didn't seem to work that way. Now there was always room for punishment in one form or another. Mercy began to feel hopeless, and just went along with whatever her parents came up with next. What difference would it make?

It had been a long time since Mercy received anything new. Things were now bought for her on an "only if needed" basis, whereas it once was on a "just because" basis. All of the things that Mercy had previously received from her father lost their place in her heart. Now the toys and things just sat in a box in her room in a corner. All of the things that once made Mercy happy were now a thing of the past. Mercy would close her eyes real tight and wished for things to return back to that way that they were, but to no avail. When she opened her eyes things were still the same. It seemed as though the only one that Mercy could count on for any happiness and comfort was the family dog. Mercy wondered whether things would ever get better for her. Who knew, maybe one day they would.

Chapter 4

MINISTRY MOMENT

Psalm 12:5 NLT, "The Lord replies, 'I have seen violence done to the helpless, and I have heard the groans of the poor. Now I will rise up to rescue them, as they have longed for me to do.'"

Even as children we go through a lot. Sometimes to us things may seem hopeless. But just know that whatever you may have experienced as a child it was only to get you prepared for your adult life. Children's minds are like sponges; they absorb so much. What our minds absorbed as children can be a stepping stone for what is to come in our future. Just know that you were not alone, and what the enemy meant for bad God can turn that situation around and use it for your good, no matter how awful the experience. If you are having any ill feelings that you may not be able to get rid of because of your past, give it to God and He will show you how to channel that pain into prosperity.

V

School of Hard Knocks

Now Mercy was in a world filled with pain and unhappiness, something she thought she would never have to experience again. It seemed as though wherever she turned there was some form of maltreatment. There was always someone waiting to cause harm to Mercy in one way or another. Mercy began to feel like she was a burden everywhere that she went. No more daddy's little girl. Mercy thought whether she even mattered to her father anymore. It seemed like Joseph Sr. became accustomed to beating Mercy. No matter how small the incident was, he would use the opportunity to beat her. He had a famous line that he would say often, which was, "This is going to hurt me more than it hurts you." On one of these many occasions, while he was hitting Mercy, her screams could be heard outside. The neighborhood children began to gather downstairs in Mercy's front yard because Mercy's voice could be heard coming from her bedroom window upstairs. And if that wasn't embarrassing enough, Mercy's dad took her downstairs, put her outside on the porch so that the children could tease her and make fun of her for getting a beating. As time went on the beatings and punishments got worse. Mercy was beginning to wonder about her mere existence.

It seemed as though as soon as she would get comfortable somewhere some form of pain would replace the comfort. "What a cold and lonely world," thought Mercy. It was like her whole world came crashing down around her. Mercy began to be withdrawn and kept to herself as much as she possibly could. Now it seemed as though the only time Mercy smiled was when she was at school among her classmates. School became a safe haven for Mercy. She hated when the weekends came because then she would have to spend the entire day at home with no relief from whatever her parents decided to throw her way, whether it was punishments, chores, beatings, or more. From the outside you would never be able to tell that anything was wrong with Mercy because she hid her pain very well. Not only that, but she also didn't tell anyone about what was taking place at home. One day during the yearly scoliosis screening Mercy's secret was discovered. While examining Mercy's spine, a nurse noticed some scars on Mercy's back. Mercy hadn't been aware of the marks on her back. After the exam the nurse and the school staff took Mercy into the office to find out the nature of the scars.

Although Mercy was afraid of what might happen when she returned home, she told the truth when asked where the scars came from. Mercy informed the nurse that she was getting beatings at home. Mercy was not allowed to return to class and her father was called. When Joseph Sr. arrived the school staff questioned him about the beatings, and to Mercy's surprise, he admitted that he had been beating her. The school staff informed him that if the beatings continued Mercy would be removed from the home and he would be arrested. Joseph Sr. agreed to stop the beatings and he left the school. Although Mercy was afraid, she was also relieved that the beatings were going to stop. When Mercy returned home from school, she didn't know what to expect. To her amazement, the rest of the evening went relatively well. A few days had passed when out of the blue a new form of punishment started. Now that Joseph Sr. could no longer beat Mercy, he began starving her. Joseph Sr. knew that there would be no scars from this form of punishment. There were different lengths of time that Mercy was kept from food. Sometime it would be for two or three days, or sometimes it would be a week before Mercy was allowed to eat. Sometimes the only meal Mercy had was during lunch at school.

During the periods when she was being punished with no food, while outside, Mercy would go to a friend's house and ask for something to eat. Her friends would sneak her things like crackers and cookies. There were also different ways that Mercy's father chose to execute the punishments when it came to food. Sometime Mercy was made to stay in her room during dinner, but there were times when Mercy was called to the dinner table but was not allowed to eat the food in front of her. She would have to sit at the table while everyone else ate and stare at the food. Being that it couldn't be seen on the outside, this form of punishment seemed to work for Joseph Sr. No one at school or anywhere else knew what Mercy was going through, but God knew. Another form of punishment that Joseph Sr. used was taking Mercy out of her bed. When Joseph Sr. did this, he would put a hard army cot in the laundry room with no pillows or blanket, and place it in the area where the dogs slept, and that's where Mercy was made to sleep. Even though all of these things were taking place, Mercy was still able to smile. As time went on, different forms of punishment would be given.

Mercy woke up to a beautiful summer day. The day seemed perfect. Mercy was happy to see such a nice day. "Maybe something good would happen for me today," or so she thought. Joseph Sr. had purchased a new outfit for Mercy to wear on this day. Mercy was so excited that maybe things were beginning to change for her. After she put the outfit on, Joseph Sr. said, "We are going out for a little while." "Things couldn't get any better, thought Mercy. It was beginning to feel like old times. With happiness and excitement, Mercy thanked her father for the outfit and got into the car. Mercy didn't say too much for fear that she would ruin the day. After lunch, Joseph Sr. pulled up in front of a barber shop. Mercy felt really special at the thought that she would get to go watch her father get his haircut. Joseph Sr. took Mercy's hand and led her inside the barber shop. They waited for a barber to become available. As soon as the opportunity arrived, Joseph Sr. had Mercy get into the barber's chair. Happy and confused, Mercy sat in the chair and wondered why she was in the chair instead of her father. Joseph Sr. had the barber cut all of Mercy's hair off. After the barber finished, Mercy looked into the mirror and her heart sank. In complete shock and unbelief, Mercy rode home with her father in complete silence, no longer feeling like the pretty little girl she once was. Mercy returned home and went straight to her room. Upon her return, her stepmother opened the door to her room, looked at Mercy, and laughed. All Mercy could do was cry. Mercy wondered what would make her father do such a thing.

Later on that same evening, Mercy found out that her stepmother told her father that she didn't know how to do Mercy's hair, and that's why her father had her hair cut. Now, when Mercy returned to school on Monday, the children laughed and teased her because of her hair. Some of the children told Mercy that she looked like a boy. This was just another thing that Mercy had to deal with on top of what she was already experiencing at home. Day in and day out, Mercy was being punished in one way or another. "When will it end?" thought Mercy. "When will it end?"

Chapter 5

MINISTRY MOMENT

II Corinthians 1:3–4 AMP, "Blessed be the God and Father of our Lord Jesus Christ, the father of sympathy and the God of every comfort, Who comforts us in every trouble so that we may also be able to comfort those who are in any kind of trouble or distress, with the comfort with which we ourselves are comforted by God."

When we experience distress in our life, we are to use it as a learning tool. God never promised that life would be easy, but He did say he would never leave us, nor forsake us. Jesus came through for the world so that we could live life more abundantly. Whatever it is that you have gone through or are currently going through, just know that you are doing it for someone else, someone who maybe experiencing similar circumstances and will need to be encouraged and comforted. You have a job to do. Share your experience and how God brought you through. Be a blessing in someone's life. Reach one, teach one.

VI

The New Addition

Some months went by and it came to be known that Karen was expecting her and Joseph Sr.'s first child. During this time, whatever Karen couldn't or wouldn't do, Mercy was made to do. After the baby was born, Mercy had to pick up where she left off with her stepsister. Now Mercy had a little brother to help look after. She had to resume her chores with the dirty diapers and more. A couple of months after the arrival of the new baby, the family moved to a new house that Joseph Sr. had built. The new house was beautiful and much larger than the old house. Mercy thought, well, maybe since the family moved things would get better. But on the contrary, things didn't change at all but became worse. Along with all of the other chores that Mercy had now, she had to babysit the children too. The bad part about this situation was Mercy was a child herself. Mercy's father and his wife would go out on a regular basis and leave Mercy at home with the children. This was a scary situation because Mercy didn't know how to properly care for the children.

One day, during one of their ventures, Mercy's brother began to cry. This seemed to go on for hours. With no way to reach her parents, Mercy became very afraid because there was nothing that she could do to stop the baby from crying. Mercy tried everything that she knew, from changing the baby's diaper to giving him a bottle, but nothing worked. She even laid him down and began patting his back, but he continued to cry. It felt like hours before her parents returned, but finally they were home. The baby was still crying when they arrived. Assuming that the baby was harmed in some way, Joseph Sr. became very angry with Mercy. Mercy explained to her father that she had given the baby some medication in hopes that it would stop him from crying. The medication made the baby ill and he had to be hospitalized. Not trying to see things from Mercy's side, Karen took Mercy to the bus stop, bought a one-way ticket to New York, and put Mercy on the bus alone. Mercy had to ride from Louisville, Kentucky to New York. She traveled for two days with no food, no money, and no adult supervision. Her parents didn't even provide her with a suitcase. She had to carry her clothes in a clear plastic bag.

Finally, after what seemed like an eternity, Mercy reached her destination safely. Mercy's aunt Martha was there waiting when she arrived. The very first thing that her aunt did was take her to get something to eat. Mercy was so hungry she devoured the food in front of her in no time at all. It was one of the best meals that Mercy had ever had. Aunt Martha took Mercy to her house, and there she stayed for two weeks. While there, Aunt Martha took Mercy shopping for all new clothes and the other necessities that she needed. While staying with her aunt, Mercy received a lot of love and attention. Mercy began to feel like a different child being away from her father and all of the maltreatment that she was receiving. Mercy was very conscious of her surroundings. She was very careful about everything that she said or did for fear of being punished. Mercy began to open up to her aunt about the way that she was being punished by her father. Mercy's aunt had a sympathetic ear and a kind heart. She promised Mercy that she had nothing to worry about while she was staying with her.

Aunt Martha became very angry about the awful treatment that Mercy had received at the hands of her father and his wife. Aunt Martha felt so helpless. All she could do was protect Mercy and give her the best care while she was staying with her. The two weeks went by so fast, and now it was time for Mercy to go back to her grandmother. Mercy didn't want to go back because of the awful things that her grandfather had done to her. Mercy knew that this was one secret that she would never tell. Aunt Martha escorted Mercy all the way back to her grandparents. This trip was scary because this was where it all began for Mercy, but now she would have to go it alone.

Chapter 6

MINISTRY MOMENT

Romans 15:3, "For Christ did not please Himself; but as it is written, 'The reproaches and abuses of those who reproached and abused you fell on Me.'"

This is letting you know that Christ took all of our hurt and pain on Himself. There is nothing that we have gone through or are going through that Christ has not already taken care of. Now it is our job to take that situation and circumstance and use it to help someone else. We are to bear one another's burdens. So the same way God helped you, now it is your turn to pay it forward and help someone else. God gives us grace (unmerited favor) to make it through our situations and circumstances. Take a minute and look back at where you were and look at where you are now. God did not bring you this far to let you go.

VII

Full Circle

Having Mercy back at home was a great pleasure and help to her grandmother. All Mercy could do was remember what was going on before she left to go live with her father. Being back in this apartment made Mercy feel so afraid and alone because she was now there by herself. It seemed as though Mercy's life had come full circle in such a short period of time. Mercy tried to think of good things, such as being back with her grandmother, whom she loved dearly and who loved her the same way. Mercy thought maybe she might even be lucky enough to see her mother and maybe her mother had gotten better and could take care of her now. Another thing that Mercy was glad about was there was food and she could eat as much as she wanted. Being able to eat was also a plus about being back at her grandparents' house. Her grandparents might not have had a lot, but they did have food. This thought seemed to cheer Mercy up somewhat. Mercy thanked God for these small miracles. Things seemed too good for a little while, but as life would have it, these good times didn't last for long.

Mercy began to get settled into being back up north. Grandpa couldn't wait to pick up where he left off. Being a little bit older now and a little wiser, Mercy was able to think of ways to stay out of her grandfather's presence as much as possible. She would stay beside her grandmother as much as she could. Whenever her grandmother would leave the house to go to her job at the Laundromat, Mercy would go with her. Because Mercy's grandmother didn't know what was going on, she would leave her in the house. It wasn't too long before Grandpa started being his old self once again. This time Mercy wasn't the lookout, she was the target. He would look at her sometimes with hunger and contempt in his eyes. Mercy thought to herself this would be the least of her worries. As long as she wasn't getting beaten and starved, she would be okay. Grandpa began approaching Mercy, and whenever she wouldn't give in to his advances, he would make Mercy stay in her room. While in the room, he would come by the door and say things like, "Those kids sure sound like they are having a lot of fun out there, don't they?" And then he would tease her and laugh.

Mercy never told her grandmother what was going on, so she thought that it was Mercy's idea to stay in the house. As long as Mercy went along with Grandpa's program everything was fine and she was allowed to go outside. Mercy thought this was a small price to pay for some sort of normalcy in her life. As a result of what was happening to her, Mercy didn't want to be around anyone that she knew for fear that she would get weak and spill the beans about her grandfather. Mercy would go on long walks to the park in a nearby neighborhood. While there she would watch families spending quality time together and enjoying each other. Being in this setting somehow cheered Mercy up. In her mind she would pretend that she was a part of the families by joining in and playing with them until it was time to get back to her grim reality. Most of the time, while in her room, Mercy would allow her imagination to run wild. She would imagine that she was rich, loved, and never punished or abused. Sometimes she would even imagine that men didn't exist. This was due to the fact that since her mere existence she only received hurt, pain, and abuse at the hands of men. Sometime she even wished that she was invisible so that no one anywhere could bring harm to her.

Mercy began to get tired of being punished, so she would let her grandfather have his way with her. Whenever she chose to stay in her neighborhood, the children would pick on her and challenge her to fight, but she would just walk away. Mercy got so tired of being abused in one way or another. She began to feel like that was what she was in this world for, to be everyone's punching bag. The only time that Mercy felt good was when she would leave her neighborhood, so that's what she started doing. Because she was able to get along with others pretty well, Mercy started making some new friends. In getting away from all of the negativity from her own neighborhood, she found out that the people that she met accepted her for who she was and enjoyed being around her. Another place that Mercy enjoyed was school. She never grew tired of learning new things. Now Mercy, a teenager and an eighth-grade graduate, wondered what the summer would hold for her. Mercy was very happy to learn that she would be spending some of her summer with her other grandmother in Brooklyn and some of her summer with her aunt Martha in Harlem. Mercy hated the fact that she would have to leave her grandmother's side, especially since she knew how her grandfather treated her.

There were times when Mercy's grandfather would come home drunk and begin torturing her grandmother. Mercy would be in her room listening to her grandmother cry. Mercy wanted to help her grandmother but she didn't know how. Nanny had very bad arthritis and she walked with a cane. Mercy's grandfather would make fun of her because of this. He would take her cane from her and hit her with it and laugh. He would also call her names and curse at her. Mercy would sometimes tell her grandmother to leave, but she said she was too old to try to go somewhere new, and continued on with the misery. It hurt Mercy's heart to have to leave her grandmother, but she assured her that she would be okay. With tears in her eyes, reluctantly Mercy left to begin her summer vacation.

Chapter 7

MINISTRY MOMENT

Isaiah 54:17, "But no weapon that is formed against you shall prosper, and every tongue that shall rise against you in judgment you shall show to be wrong."

The things that happen to us throughout our lives are weapons. God never said that we would live this life without going through things. He just said they wouldn't prosper, which means that you may have a few bumps, bruises, and scars but that's just evidence that you made it through. Jesus went through for us so that when we are faced with situations and circumstances we can make it through also. Jesus was our prime example of going from the pain and getting to the promise. If there be anybody who tells you that you can't do this or that, tell them what God said about you.

VIII

New York State of Mind

Mercy spent the first part of her summer with Aunt Martha. Mercy really enjoyed all the attention that received while there. While in Harlem, Mercy got to meet her other family members that she did not know. Mercy had a cousin named Lisa whom she had come to love. The two were inseparable. Lisa stayed at Aunt Martha's while Mercy was there even though she lived but a few blocks away. Lisa began to show Mercy the ropes about living in Harlem. They were privy to parties and bus rides because Aunt Martha was a member of a group called the Eastern Stars. There was always some kind of ball or trip to attend, and Aunt Martha made sure that she and the girls stayed on the go. Mercy absorbed as much about Harlem as she could while there. Aunt Martha loved having the girls with her because she didn't have any children of her own. Aunt Martha also took the girls on a shopping spree. Mercy really liked this because she didn't have many clothes and wasn't too sure she was going to get more, so she welcomed this gladly. Now it was time for Mercy to leave Aunt Martha's. This was hard because she was leaving a life that she came to love and family that she had just become acquainted with. Aunt Martha told Mercy that she was always welcome to come and visit any time she wanted. Mercy was already thinking about her next visit. Lisa came along with Aunt Martha to escort Mercy to Brooklyn, where her other grandmother lived. With a hug and kiss, Lisa and Aunt Martha headed back to Harlem.

Mercy's other grandmother, Jeffy, as she was lovingly referred to by her grandchildren, was the mother of Mercy's mom. After arriving at Jeffy's house, Mercy worked on getting settled in so that she could start on the second part of her summer vacation. Even though it was also in the city, Mercy noticed that there was a difference between Brooklyn and Harlem. It was like living in two different worlds. Brooklyn seemed to be just a little bit slower than Harlem when it came to city living, at least in Mercy's eyes. Mercy couldn't wait to see her other family members whom she hadn't seen in years. Mercy didn't know what to expect. It was nice because all of the family members lived in walking distance of each other. During her visit, Mercy got reacquainted with her aunts, uncles, and cousins. All of Mercy's family treated her well. This made Mercy feel like she was worthy to be loved. No one yelled, hit, or punished Mercy while she was there. Mercy was able to enjoy herself while she was there. She was able to go outside with her cousins, and she even had money that was given to her with no strings attached. Mercy was also able to go on bus rides to different places while there. Her family had a club called Family and Friends, and they would give neighborhood bus outings to different places. Mercy got to see a whole different world once she left New Jersey.

Mercy hated the thought that she would eventually have to leave all of the fun and good times behind, so she decided to have as much fun as she possibly could while there. The reason Mercy had to go back was her father had custody of her and wanted her to stay with his mother. Every day was another adventure to look forward to. You never knew what was going to happen, either while in the house or outside. Sometimes people would bring large speakers to the parks and play music. People would come from everywhere just to dance and have a good time. Mercy loved when this happened. Her cousin Shcora, who was the same age as she was, would come to Jeffy's house, get Mercy, and they would run as fast as they could to the place where the music was coming from. Once there they would join the crowd in dancing and enjoying the music also. Sometimes Shcora would come get Mercy and go skating. This was something else that Mercy really enjoyed doing. Mercy didn't have a care in the world while visiting with her family. It was one good time after another. Mercy noticed that her cousin was very independent when it came to traveling. They traveled by bus and by subway to get to different places. Jeffy was a seamstress, so she was very talented when it came to making clothes for her grandchildren. This was very nice, especially in the summer. The children would have unique fashions to wear and everyone complimented Jeffy on her talent. It seemed as though time was flying, and soon it would be time for Mercy to return to New Jersey. She never told anyone, not even her cousin, what was taking place at her other grandmother's house for fear of getting in trouble or worse. She tried to push these unpleasant thoughts as far back in her mind as she could. Mercy continued enjoying her family and friends as much as she possibly could and not think about anything else but having a good time.

Mercy began to get depressed because there was only a week left until she would have to return to the loving care of her grandmother and the cruel hands of her grandfather. Mercy began to become withdrawn, and when asked what was wrong, she said she didn't want to leave. As with Aunt Martha, Mercy was always welcome to visit with her family anytime. It was just the fact of when that hurt her. The day finally came when it was time for Mercy to return to New Jersey. Her cousins helped her to the bus station and they said their goodbyes. While the bus was pulling out, Mercy began to cry because no one knew what lay ahead of her when she returned home. All she would have were pleasant memories of all the things that she and her family did while she was with them. She focused on this while on the bus until she drifted off to sleep. When she awoke, she was in New Jersey and the first face that she saw smiling at her was her grandmother waiting for her to get off the bus. Nanny couldn't wait to hear about her summer and all that she did while she was gone. If only it was just the two of them, then life would really be sweet, thought Mercy.

Chapter 8

MINISTRY MOMENT

Ecclesiastes 7:8, "The end of a thing is better than its beginning."

If you feel like you want to give up and throw in the towel, don't! God has great things in store for you. According to God's word, your latter shall be greater than your beginning. This is because God is the Alpha and the Omega, which means He is the beginning and end of all things. He is preparing you for greater. Everything that you have gone through was to prepare you for now. God wrote the book. He doesn't make mistakes. Don't let the pangs of life get you down. As long as you live there will be trials and tribulations, but there is nothing that you and God cannot handle together. Put your hand in God's hands and let Him lead you into your destiny that He has designed just for you.

IX

For Better or Worse

Mercy's grandparents moved out of the city to the country part of New Jersey. Despite all that was going on with her, Mercy's grades were good. Mercy was now a sophomore in high school and she even had a seasonal job. Her job and her good grades gave Mercy a sense of accomplishment. She felt like anything was possible. Things were beginning to look up for her. Now she was able to give her grandparents money to help buy things for the house. Mercy was even able to buy her own clothes for school. Times changed even though her situation had not. Mercy became more outgoing. She was even on the drill team at school and began to make new friends in and outside of school. Mercy even tried her hand at dating. Mercy seemed to enjoy life a lot more now than she ever had. Maybe it was because she was getting older and closer to escaping all that had plagued her up until this time in her life. She worked for a well-known amusement park. Whenever a new ride was introduced to the park, the owners would shut the park down to the public and let the employees enjoy the ride first. Mercy enjoyed these times because it gave her time to hang out with her friends and have fun.

Mercy missed traveling to New York to spend time with her family, so she enjoyed her summer the best way that she could. It seemed like now that they were living in the country part of New Jersey no one wanted to travel to see them, and because of her job Mercy couldn't do any traveling either. So she decided to make the best of things the only way she knew how. Mercy tried to keep up with all the goings on outside of work as much as possible. Even when she didn't have to work, she would get a ride to the park just to hang out. Pretty soon the park would be closing for the season and it would be back to school. Mercy saved some of the money that she earned so that way even when she wasn't working she would still have some money to spend as she pleased. Mercy didn't know what she wanted to do once she graduated. She didn't know if she would attend college or just get a job. She put those thoughts on the back burner for a while and continued putting her best foot forward in school and learning all that she could while she was there. There was a group of girls that didn't like Mercy because she was becoming very popular at school. They would always make comments about her as she walked the halls but Mercy didn't pay them any attention. One day they decided to have some fun at Mercy's expense. The girls got one of the girls in their group to harass Mercy, and Mercy tried to ignore the girl. This continued on for a while until the girl pushed Mercy. This didn't bother Mercy. She just continued getting ready for her gym class. The girl pushed Mercy again while the other girls laughed at what was going on, but Mercy ignored her yet again. The girl pushed Mercy for a third time, only this time before she knew it Mercy punched the girl and busted her lip. The other girls looked like they were in shock at what just took place. Mercy got suspended for a week, but after that she never had to prove herself ever again.

Mercy went back to being the nice girl that she was but now the word got out that she could fight. This made Mercy feel bad. She didn't want people to get the wrong impression about her and who she really was. It seemed as though all of those years of abuse and bullying created an anger inside Mercy that she didn't know she was capable of having. Mercy tried to stay out of sight as much as possible to diffuse any more run-ins with the wrong people. It took everything in her to keep quiet even when things were going in the wrong direction. Mercy began to throw herself into her schoolwork and also her chores at home. This seemed to help Mercy redirect the anger that was trying to rise up inside her. Mercy made it through the rest of her sophomore year with ease. Not only that, but she was also promoted to the eleventh grade. Mercy was so happy once again; she accomplished something. "Wow," thought Mercy, "before you know it I will be a high school graduate." No more outbursts of anger. Mercy tried to keep pleasant and positive thoughts in her mind. Mercy was going to take life by the horns and make something out of her life. Out of all of the negativity surrounding her life, something good was sure to be on its way. "Now to start planning my future. I've been down for too long, there's no place else to go but up." And with that, Mercy looked forward to starting a new chapter in her life.

Life really was getting better for Mercy. Grandpa didn't bother her as much as he used to. Nanny seemed to be happier since the move even though Grandpa still gave her a hard time sometimes. Even Aunt Lula and Uncle Foreman moved down the street from them. Now Mercy could also go and visit with them. It was beginning to feel like old times in a sense. The only thing that was missing was her brother and sister. Mercy went back to her job at the amusement park. She put in for a different department when she returned, and to her surprise she got it. Mercy liked trying new things, and that's what she did. She tried to learn as much as she could about how the park operated and how many departments there were. Each chance that she got, she tried her hand at something else. Who knew, maybe she would get into the management field. The sky was the limit for her. All Mercy did was work and save. She wasn't too interested in going out like she was at one time. Mercy was trying to keep a level head when it came to her future. Only God knew what was in store for her at this point in her life. Mercy paid close attention to everything that went on around her, making sure she didn't miss anything. Now she took on one more task, the task of learning to drive. Mercy had received her permit while in school. The lessons didn't go too well because no one had the patience to teach her, but Mercy never gave up trying to learn. She even snuck out her grandfather's car a couple of times in order to get some road time.

Chapter 9

MINISTRY MOMENT

Jeremiah 29:11, "For I know the thoughts that I think towards you, says the Lord, thoughts of peace and not of evil, to give you a future and a hope."

God only wants the best for us. Despite what we may face during our lifetime, God is on our side, cheering us on through the storms of life. God is the author who wrote the book of our lives. He already paved the way for us; all we have to do is walk out the pages from beginning to end. He knows that we are going to come through with flying colors. All we have to do is take His hand and let Him lead the way as we go from trial to triumph, victim to victor. All things are possible through God. Only what you do for Christ will last. So don't let the hard work and sacrifice of Jesus go to waste. Stand up and brush the dirt of life off. Get in the word and find out what God would have for you to do. Let His word transform you from the inside out.

X

An Offer I Could Not Refuse

Now summer was here once again and it was the summer before Mercy's senior year. Mercy had no idea what she was going to do once school was out, but just the mere fact that she made it this far in life was truly a blessing. One weekend before Mercy was to go back to her summer job at the amusement park, her family had a cookout. Some of the family from up north came down to visit. One of the family members that came to visit was Mercy's uncle Danny. Danny was Grandpa's son. Danny was married and had three children. The family gathering turned out to be very nice and relaxing. It was just what Mercy needed. Mercy had been contemplating leaving her grandparents' house. The only thing was she had no idea how to leave or where she would go once she did. Right out of the blue, Danny offered Mercy a babysitting job for the summer. He told her that she would not have to worry about anything; he and his wife would take care of her. This job offer seemed to be the answer that Mercy was looking for in her plight to leave her grandparents' house. Aunt Lula warned Mercy not to go anywhere with Danny. Aunt Lula knew Danny all too well, but what she didn't know was that Mercy was trying to get away from her grandfather.

All Mercy could think about was escaping the pain of her current situation. So with that in mind, Mercy was off for the summer to make some money and have some fun, or so she thought. Things seemed to be going pretty well in the beginning, but after a couple of weeks Mercy could see why Aunt Lula warned her not to go. Danny began making frequent visits to the room that Mercy shared with the children. It started out with him touching her, and it escalated very fast to him penetrating her. Mercy was afraid to tell anyone for fear that no one would believe her. She was also afraid because she had no other place to stay while she was up north. Mercy began to think back on what her aunt was trying to tell her. Now she felt like she was between a rock and a hard place. There were situations on both sides; Grandpa on one side, and Danny on the other, and neither situation was good. Mercy didn't know it at the time, but God had a plan. A short while after the visits started, Mercy began to get sick in the mornings. What Mercy didn't know was that she was now pregnant with her uncle's baby. After all that Mercy had already endured throughout her life, now she had yet another issue to worry about. When Mercy found out what was causing her sickness, she became worried. The first thing that Mercy thought was, "What am I going to do?" She thought of trying to lie her way out of it, but that was no good because she had the kids all day, and when she didn't have them she was in the house. Mercy was stuck between a rock and a hard place again. Not only did she not make the money that she thought she was going to make, but now she was also pregnant. "What am I going to do?" thought Mercy. "What in the world am I going to do?"

Not too long after Mercy's condition came to light, Danny's wife wanted to know who the other party was in the situation. Mercy was so afraid, she just began naming names. After listening for a while, Casandra knew that she was lying. Mercy grew tired of lying and decided to come clean about everything. Once the truth came out, Mercy was made to leave Danny's house, but not before he had a chance to have a word with her. Danny took Mercy on a late night walk. Once he got to his destination, he told Mercy that he would kill her for ruining his marriage. He took her to the end of a wooden pier and threatened to throw her off. He must have thought against it because the next thing that Mercy knew she was on the ground, being sexually assaulted. After Danny got his point across, he got up and just left Mercy there. Feeling helpless and worthless, Mercy got up and made her way back to the house. Mercy couldn't wait until daybreak. Although she didn't have a place to stay, she knew that she would be better off away from there. Starting out walking, she tried to see if any of her old neighborhood friends would be able to help her. Being back down to zero with nothing and no place to go, she walked until she came in contact with one of her childhood friends. Mercy began to tell her friend Leslie what had been going on with her. Leslie took Mercy to her house and told her mother and asked if Mercy could stay with them for a while. Leslie's mom let Mercy stay with them. In the meantime, Leslie tried to help Mercy find her mom. A month went by, and just when it seemed hopeless, they found Mercy's mom. Leslie and Mercy took a trip to a neighboring city to see Mercy's mom. Mercy's mom seemed happy to see Mercy. As far as Mercy could see, not much had changed with her mother and her addiction to alcohol.

Leslie and Mercy sat down with Mercy's mom and explained the situation. After talking with them, Mercy's mom said that it wasn't up to her whether Mercy could stay with her or not. Mercy's mom lived with her boyfriend William. She did allow them to stay until he came home. Mercy's mom told William the situation and asked if it would be okay if Mercy stayed with them, and he said she could. Happy and relieved, Mercy got what little clothes she had and moved into her mother's place. Once she began to get settled in, this arrangement did not come easy. William quickly let Mercy know what he expected from her. This didn't seem too hard because Mercy stayed in the house by herself the majority of the time. Mercy's mom asked her what she planned to do about her current situation. Mercy thought about getting an abortion but did not have the money to do so. Dorothy went to the store and bought some turpentine. Mercy's mom began giving Mercy turpentine and sugar in hopes of making Mercy abort the baby. As horrible as it tasted, Mercy went along with this process for a few days. After this plan failed, Mercy knew that she didn't have a choice but to keep the baby. Once it was finally settled that Mercy was going to have the baby, Mercy's mom helped Mercy get some resources to help her in her situation.

Being pregnant was the worst feeling ever. Mercy was basically bedridden for a lot of the pregnancy. She couldn't even enjoy a drink of water without it coming back up. Mercy began to see a doctor for her prenatal care. Feeling weak and losing weight, Mercy thought that something was definitely wrong with her or the baby. After her initial checkup, everything was determined to be fine. Mercy's morning sickness was just an extreme case and everything else seemed to be okay. Time was flying and now Mercy was into her fourth month and began noticing the changes that were beginning to take place inside and outside of her body. Instead of Mercy being happy about becoming a mother, she was ashamed and embarrassed. Mercy thought about what events led up to her being in her current condition and all she could do was cry. Not knowing what she was going to do after the baby arrived gave Mercy a lot to think about. While all of these things were taking place, there were also the issues that Mercy began facing with William. He was also an alcoholic and had anger issues when it came to Mercy. At any time when he felt like it, he would cause a confrontation with Mercy and it resulted in him putting her out on the street. With no regard for her life or the baby that she carried, she would have to pack a bag and leave. Because her mother had no say-so when it came to the apartment, whatever William said had to be done or else. This behavior seemed to go off and on whenever he felt like it. It was bad enough that he had monopolized all of her mother's time when she was home, but now to have to go through being homeless off and on was just too much to bear. Once again she had to call on the only person that she knew would help, her friend Leslie. Feeling like a burden, Mercy did whatever she could do to stay out of everyone's way. Whenever she had to ask Leslie and her family for help, she would try to stay no longer than a week at the most, by then William would usually have cooled down enough to let Mercy back in until he decided to go on another rampage.

It was almost time for Mercy to deliver. Aunt Martha gave Mercy a surprise baby shower, and to her surprise, Nanny and Grandpa were there. This made Mercy feel sort of special. Her cousins from Brooklyn were there also. Mercy couldn't remember when she felt so much love. The baby shower turned out to be beautiful. The only thing that put a damper on the occasion was Mercy's mom. Before the shower, Mercy's mom promised Mercy that she wouldn't drink and spoil her day. This didn't turn out at all the way Mercy had hoped. Not only did she have to carry the majority of her gifts home, but now she had to help her mother also. Her cousins pitched in to help her and he mom get to their bus safely. On the ride home, Mercy thought about how this situation was going to affect her after she had the baby. Mercy was now nineteen and about to become a mother any day. Excitement and fear filled Mercy as time passed. Each day she woke up wondering whether this was going to be the day. Having gone through three false alarms, Mercy couldn't wait to get this delivery over with. Finally, it was time for the delivery. Mercy was at home alone when her water broke. Mercy's mom and William met Mercy at the hospital to visit while she was in labor. Even during this important occasion her mother and William couldn't stay sober. Instead, they came up, made a small disturbance, and then left. Mercy, not knowing what to do, was left to give birth by herself. Thank God for small favors. There was a young a couple nearby having a baby at the same time as Mercy. The husband saw that Mercy was alone and came over to talk to her. Thirteen and a half hours later, Mercy gave birth to a 6 lbs., 7 1/2 oz. baby boy.

Chapter 10

MINISTRY MOMENT

Proverbs 3:5–6, "Trust in the Lord with all of your heart and lean not unto your own understanding. In all your ways acknowledge Him and He will direct your paths."

When our situations look impossible, God already has the master plan in place. We become fearful because we can't see our way out. Do not despair. God will work out your situation and your circumstances if you look to Him for all that you need. When things look hopeless, put your hope in the one that died for us, Jesus Christ. We were created for a purpose, and when we give our life to God, His glory can be revealed throughout our lives. Don't let your situations dictate to you. Know that God is the creator of all. He knows what's going to happen before it even begins. Cast your cares on Him because He cares for you.

XI

New Beginnings

Motherhood felt very nice after all of the hardships that Mercy had suffered throughout her life. Maybe, just maybe, she could start all over, giving her child everything that she did not receive while growing up. Mercy didn't know how, but she was determined to protect her son from any harm or maltreatment she had experienced. Coming from where she came from, all she knew how to do was love. She found so much joy each time she looked into her son's eyes. Mercy never looked at him out of the eyes of abuse and molestation but looked at him through the eyes of her heart. Living with Mom and William proved to be challenging because they tried to take over when it came to little David. They would take him in the room with them and keep him for hours. One morning when Mercy awoke she noticed that David was gone. Beginning to panic, she went out to see if maybe her mother and William were sitting outside with the baby. She did not see them anywhere around the area. The phone rang. When Mercy answered the phone, it was her mother telling her that they were in New York visiting Jeffy and David was with them. Mercy hung up the phone and was very upset. Not only had they not invited her to come along, but they also took her son without asking her if it was okay. Mercy spent the day worrying about how they were taking care of the baby. Were they feeding him correctly? Were they changing him properly? Were they sober? All of these questions tortured Mercy until they arrived back home with David. Mercy was so happy and relieved to have her son back in her arms, she began to laugh and cry at the same time.

Mercy confronted her mom and William about taking the baby without her knowledge. She let them know that she didn't appreciate it, and next time they could let her know so that she could come with them. William said they didn't think that it would be a problem taking the baby out for a while. Mercy could see that they had been drinking while they had her son with them. Mercy's mom hid behind William's words instead of saying anything on her own behalf. Mercy took David in their room and closed the door. Afraid of any further confrontation, the rest of the evening was spent in silence between her and them. Each new day brought about a learning experience. Being a single parent taught Mercy a lot of new things. One was that traveling was no longer that easy, especially with a baby and a stroller. Independence was definitely a must. You must always prepare for the unexpected. Even though she was a teenager, Mercy had to grow up and mature a little faster than she would have liked to since now she was responsible for another life besides her own. Mercy tried to stay out of her mother and William's way as much as possible, so she spent a majority of her time in Bayonne. She would visit with her friends and their families before returning home. She thought this was a good plan because she didn't know if William would go on one of his power trips and tell her she had to leave. If this was to happen, she was definitely taking her son with her. Mercy didn't like the feeling of walking on eggshells all of the time when it came to William's house. Mercy did whatever she had to do to keep a roof over her son's head until something else came through for her.

Good times seemed to only last so long with William. Mercy's mom and William came in, and not even five minutes after they were home, William called Mercy out of her room. William informed Mercy that she would have to leave because she was causing too much chaos in the house. Mercy didn't understand how this could be because she stayed to herself most of the time. Not only that, but they never interacted with her, and when they did they were intoxicated. Mercy didn't put up an argument or try to protest. She began to pack up what she could and she and the baby left. "How could life be so cruel," thought Mercy. Now she had to find a place to stay for her and her son. The only person right now that she knew would be of help to her was her friend Leslie. Feeling like a great big burden but not having a choice, she asked Leslie if they could stay with her and her family once again. Thank God that Leslie's mom understood what Mercy was going through and had compassion for her. Leslie's mom treated Mercy like she was one of her own children. While at Leslie's house, Mercy began to look for a place of her own to stay. Not too far away from Leslie lived a cousin of Nanny's named Patricia. Mercy went to Cousin Patricia's house and found out that she had a room for rent. "Wow!" thought Mercy. When Mercy explained her situation to Cousin Patricia and told her what was going on, Patricia allowed Mercy to move in and rent the room. Mercy used her public assistance money to pay Patricia for the room. Cousin Patricia was an older lady who lived alone. She seemed to be nice, at least in the beginning. Mercy began to feel good, with a sense of accomplishment. This was the first grownup decision that Mercy had to make for her and her son's wellbeing. David would never know what it felt like to be unwanted, unloved, or homeless no matter what Mercy had to endure.

Mercy began to get settled once again, this time in Cousin Pat's house. Once she had gotten settled, Mercy knew she had to think about the future for her and her son. The first thing that Mercy found was someone to care for her son. The lady lived in the same building as Cousin Pat. Thank God for that, and she didn't charge her a whole lot of money to keep David. After getting acquainted with the babysitter, Mercy felt like her son would be in good hands. Now after that was taken care of, the next thing that Mercy did was enroll herself into business school. This was something that excited Mercy because she liked to type and she was very good when it came to dealing with people. Although she didn't graduate from high school, Mercy seemed to pick up what was being taught very quickly. Mercy began to have a whole new outlook on life because of what she was learning. This was a new chapter in her life that she welcomed gladly. Going to school seemed to be slightly challenging to Mercy. After school was finished, she couldn't wait to get home to her son. She missed him terribly while she was in school but what she was working on now would help them both in the long run. Pretty soon things at Cousin Pat's house began to go sour. Now why didn't this surprise Mercy? Once at home she would have to fix dinner for Cousin Pat and clean up whatever mess Cousin Pat made while she was gone. "Why is this happening yet again?" thought Mercy. Although she was tired, she went ahead and did what needed to be done without saying a word.

Day in and day out, Mercy would go to school, come home, and cook and clean. Mercy thought to herself Cousin Pat should be paying her instead of her having to pay Cousin Pat. As life would have it, once again Mercy could see that this arrangement was not going to last long. Cousin Pat began to get very demanding with what she wanted Mercy to do in the house. Mercy tried everything that she could to make Cousin Pat happy but nothing seemed to work. One Saturday out of nowhere Cousin Pat called Mercy and began to accuse her of not doing anything. She also began acting very nasty to Mercy. Before Mercy knew what was going on, Cousin Pat told Mercy that she had to leave. Mercy couldn't, for the life of her, understand what was going on. "Why does this keep happening to me? I try to do my best everywhere I go," she thought to herself. "Now what am I going to do?" Just when it looked like she was making progress in her life, here was something else to knock her back down again. All Mercy could do was gather whatever she could from Cousin Pat's house and go back to Leslie's family. Leslie's mom took care of the baby while Mercy and Leslie went back to retrieve the rest of her belongings. Mercy was so hurt and discouraged because she wouldn't be able to finish school like she had planned. Mercy was stuck between a rock and a hard place again. Thank God for the help of Leslie and her family. While there, Mercy and Leslie put their heads together to come up with a plan for Mercy and David. "There has to be something good coming my way," thought Mercy. "I just wish I knew when."

Mercy stayed with Leslie and her family a little longer than she had hoped to this time. The last resort that she had at this particular time was to try and stay with her mother and William for as long as she could. This was going to be a very hard pill to swallow, thought Mercy, but it was worth a shot. Traveling back to Jersey City, Mercy yelled up to her mother's window to see if she was home. Without getting an answer, Mercy sat on the steps and waited for either her mother or William to get home. Although it seemed like forever, finally she could see her mother coming down the street. Mercy could already tell from the way her mother was walking that she had been drinking. Mercy's mom smiled when she saw Mercy and David. Mercy followed her mom in the house. At first Mercy tried to pretend that she was just there to visit, but after a while she confessed that she needed a place to stay. Mercy's mom said that if it was up to her it wouldn't be a problem but she would have to talk to William. Mercy was nervous about what William would say. After talking to William, he said that she could stay there but he also let her know that this was just temporary. At this point, Mercy agreed in order to buy some time for her and her son. Mercy decided to leave some things at Leslie's house just in case. So with all being said and done, at least for now Mercy moved back in with her mother and William.

Leslie came up with a proposal for Mercy's housing issues. Since Leslie had a job and Mercy had income coming in also, she asked Mercy if she wanted to be her roommate. This proposal couldn't come at a better time, especially since her living situation was temporary. They agreed to share living expenses. The only thing that they didn't know was where they were going to live. Their search ended up the street from Mercy's mom's house. There was a rooming house up the street from her and there was a vacancy. Mercy and Leslie went up the block to inquire about the room and the rent. The meeting with the landlord went very well, and now Mercy and Leslie were roommates. Mercy felt very secure in this decision as Leslie had always been there for Mercy whenever she needed her, even now. It just so happened that Mercy's mom was getting new furniture, so she gave Mercy her old furniture. The room was big enough to make two rooms out of it. Part of the room was the living room and the other part was where Mercy and David slept. Mercy was excited about her newfound independence. Leslie was only there sometimes at night; she still stayed with her mom most of the time. Mercy was very grateful to Leslie for helping her. She would forever be in debt to her. Maybe, just maybe, all of the bad times could be put far behind her as only learning experiences instead of roadblocks to her future.

Chapter 11

MINISTRY MOMENT

Psalm 9:18, "For the needy will not be forgotten; the hopes of the poor will not always be crushed."

If you are in a needy situation, just know that God will meet you right where you are. He is working on your behalf even though you can't see it. God is with you in whatever situation you are in. You are not alone. God is going to meet you right where you are if you let Him. Give God your hopes and your dreams; most importantly, give Him your life. Watch Him take what looks like nothing and make something beautiful. You are God's art work, His masterpiece. Let Him put you on His potter's wheel to make, shape, and mold your life into what He wants it to be.

XII

You live and You learn

Being a single parent wasn't an easy job. Being the only adult in the house made things difficult sometimes. Mercy now had to learn how to do everything, not only for herself, but she now also had this little person depending on her for everything that he needed. No more running to Mom for answers; Mercy just had to figure things out on her own. Traveling was the hardest because she would have the baby in one arm and the stroller in the other. There would be someone to help once in a while, but not all of the time. Sometimes it felt like she was in boot camp. A diaper bag with everything except the kitchen sink inside on her shoulder, along with the baby and the stroller, was a lot, but this was part of the life of being a single parent. Mercy would only take the bus on the weekends or if the baby had a doctor's appointment. The weather began to change. It started getting warm outside. Now Mercy and David would go outside for walks or just sit in front of the building for some time before it got dark. Mercy's mom would sneak up the street to visit her and David from time to time. For the majority of the time, it was because she had someone else that she was visiting also. Even though her mom was with William, she still longed to hang out the way she used to when Mercy was a little girl. She would come and visit with Mercy for a few minutes and then she would tell her not to tell William that she had been there if he came looking for her. Not wanting to get in the middle of their mess, Mercy did as her mother asked. The weird part was the satisfaction the she felt knowing that her mother was being unfaithful to him. Oh well, thought Mercy, and continued on with her own life.

As time went on things seemed to go pretty well now that Mercy was out of William's house. Mercy's mom would ask to keep David on the weekends, and depending on her condition when she asked, Mercy let her. Mercy's mom had started drinking when she was a teenager, so now the alcohol was a part of her life. She couldn't function without it. On one of the occasions when she didn't have David, Mercy wanted to know what all the excitement was about drinking, so she decided to try it for herself. Because she wasn't old enough to buy alcohol on her own, she had to find someone to get it for her. There was a young man that knew her mother very well. His name was Maurice. Mercy told Maurice that she wanted to get something to drink and he took her with him to purchase the alcohol. Maurice said he would teach Mercy how to drink. He purchased different types of alcohol for Mercy to try. After a while Mercy began to feel funny. Mercy tried to stand up and stumbled. This seemed funny to Mercy at the time. Maurice continued to give Mercy more alcohol. After a while, Mercy couldn't see because her eyesight was blurry. Mercy became afraid because the place where they had been drinking was not familiar. It was very late in the evening and Mercy was alone. Mercy didn't know it yet, but Maurice had left her. Mercy began to cry because not only could she not see, but she was also all alone and didn't know where she was. Mercy tried to walk, but because of the alcohol this was almost impossible. "How could Maurice leave me in this condition?" she thought. Someone saw the condition that Mercy was in and offered to help her.

Thank God for His protection. Even when we are messed up, He still has His hand on us. Mercy finally arrived home. Drunk and crying, not understanding what just happened or why, she washed up and proceeded to go to bed. As she lay there it felt like she was on a merry-go-round. Everything began to spin really fast. "This does not feel good at all," thought Mercy. The minute the room stopped spinning, Mercy began to vomit. She was very sick. Mercy didn't realize it but she was suffering from alcohol poisoning. She continued to vomit for what seemed like an eternity. Finally there was nothing left inside her and there was nothing left to do but go to sleep. When Mercy woke up she felt really bad. She had the worst headache ever and it felt like her insides had been ripped out. The sun was shining outside. It was now 2:00 p.m. the next day. There was a knock at the door. When Mercy opened the door it was her mother. Mercy's mother teased Mercy and laughed at her. She kept asking her if she wanted something to drink. Mercy didn't find this to be funny at all. Mercy told her mom what Maurice did and all her mom could do was laugh. Mercy was so upset at what happened to her last night. She couldn't believe that Maurice had put her in danger like that. She was sure going to give him a piece of her mind when she saw him again. The mere fact that her mom found this to be so funny made Mercy even angrier. William was on his way up the street with David. Mercy straightened up as much as she could under the circumstances and took her son from William. She thanked them for keeping him and went inside to clean up.

It had been some time since the drinking incident occurred. Mercy had begun to make some new friends. The people that Mercy sometimes hung out with were into all types of different things. Some of them drank. Some of them smoked marijuana. Mercy even saw one of them smoking a crack pipe. "This is not good," thought Mercy. Mercy asked a lot of questions because she was curious as to why someone would want to smoke crack or weed. The people who were doing it said they liked the way it made them feel when they smoked. Although she'd had that first bad experience with alcohol, Mercy drank a little whenever she didn't have her son with her. At least now she knew when to stop. As time went on, Mercy's curiosity got the best of her. One night while she was with some of her friends she decided to smoke some weed. With the very first try, Mercy inhaled and began to choke. Mercy was so afraid because the coughing seemed like it wasn't going to stop. Pretty soon Mercy began to feel the effects of the weed. Everything appeared to be funny. Mercy and her friends began laughing for no apparent reason. Everything seemed funny.

Mercy also began to feel paranoid. She began to feel like someone was watching her. She also began to get uncomfortable around her newfound friends. Once these feelings began to surface, Mercy made everyone go home. No one could understand what was wrong with her. Mercy told everyone that she had to work in the morning, so she was going to bed. The real reason was the weed had her so paranoid that she couldn't trust anyone, so she became afraid. After everyone left, Mercy began to feel somewhat better and started to calm down. Once she began feeling normal again, she got herself ready for bed. "Another new experience," thought Mercy. She continued to think about how the weed had made her feel. The laughing part was fun, but the paranoia was what she didn't like. David would be home soon, so Mercy cleaned up and got ready to receive her son. It was almost time for David's first birthday. Leslie helped Mercy plan a birthday party for David with Leslie's family. Mercy was turning twenty the week before David's birthday. To celebrate Mercy's birthday, Mercy and Leslie took a trip to Manhattan. They walked around Times Square, went to get something to eat, and afterward just took in all of the excitement that Manhattan had to offer. Mercy thanked Leslie's mom for watching David for her. Mercy spent the night at Leslie's family's house. Life was beginning to change in more ways than one for Mercy. "I guess life is what you make of it," thought Mercy, so she tried to stay positive.

Mercy had now experienced life on a different level. She had one experience with alcohol and a totally different experience with marijuana. She couldn't understand why people would want to walk around feeling the way these things made them feel. Why would anyone want to walk around so high that they were not aware of what was going on around them? Why would someone want to feel like they were constantly being watched or that someone was out to harm them? Mercy was quite content for now with experiencing life on different levels. Mercy wanted to focus on her and David, and that's what she did. Grateful that things didn't get any worse, Mercy didn't try anything new anytime soon. There was a church across the street from where Mercy lived. She thought about giving church a try; after all, this could be the answer to all of her life's issues. The next weekend, Mercy decided to attend a church service. The church looked scary from the outside because the building was old. Once inside she looked around and it didn't seem that bad. The music sounded good and that helped Mercy feel a little bit more comfortable. The sermon seemed to lift Mercy's spirit. After church, Mercy noticed that she knew some of the people from her childhood. They noticed her and came and spoke to her and David. Mercy felt like this was meant to be, so after talking and catching up on things Mercy decided to return the following Sunday.

Mercy began going to church on a regular basis. She even became a member of the church choir. Things began to change once again for the better, thought Mercy. She started to feel like she was actually a part of society. She was a part of something good. Pretty soon Mercy began dating. She liked to date casually. This gave Mercy a sense of control. Go out, have a good time, and go home. No commitment, just two people enjoying each other's company. This went off and on for a while. Mercy made it a rule not to introduce her dates to her son, although she did inform them that she had a child. She wasn't looking for a father for David. Now life seemed fun for Mercy. One day Mercy ran into her friends from the hospital. James and his wife Desirae had a beautiful little girl named Delilah. Mercy and Desirae would get together on weekends when they had the time. The friendship was nice and a change from the people that she hung out with in the neighborhood. They had a cute little apartment not too far away from the hospital where the children were born. On one of the visits to their house, James's brother Alfred stopped by. James didn't hesitate introducing them to each other. Mercy already knew this was a setup. Because they knew that Mercy was single, they decided to play matchmaker for her, something that Mercy didn't want or need any help with. Mercy decided to get to know Alfred. Besides, she felt a little obligated because they went out of their way to help her during her delivery.

Getting to know Alfred wasn't bad in the beginning, but things began to move a little too fast too soon, thought Mercy. Alfred was a good guy but he was looking for a commitment that Mercy wasn't ready to give. He dove in when it came to the fatherly role in David's life. They went everywhere together and spent almost every waking hour together. This was getting a little too close for comfort, thought Mercy. Seeing how things were going against her better judgment, Mercy asked her mom to watch David so that she and Alfred could go out. Alfred had a romantic evening planned for both of them. After dinner they went near the pier and watched the boats go by. Mercy was trying to slow things down before they went any further, but before she had a chance to plead her case, Alfred had already taken her back to his house. While there they listened to some music, danced, had a glass of wine, and then found themselves in a compromising position. Mercy was nervous but soon began to relax. All she could think about was the last time something like this happened to her it was being forced. Mercy fought back tears of the horrible memories that plagued her. She had to constantly tell herself to calm down, this is different. Finally the time came to an end. Alfred noticed how tense Mercy seemed and asked her if she was okay. Mercy said she was fine, just worried about being away from David too long. They got themselves together and left Alfred's house and went back to Mercy's mom's to get David. Mercy told Alfred that she had a great time but needed some time apart to think about things. He said okay, gave her a kiss, and left. Mercy thanked her mother for keeping David and headed back up the street to her place. All she could do was think about what just happened between her and Alfred and where this was going to lead them.

Ever since that night with Alfred, Mercy wasn't herself. She had been feeling a little rundown and depressed and couldn't figure out why. Mercy and David were baptized. This was another turn of events for the better in Mercy's life. She worked on her relationship with God. With all of these positive things happening, why was Mercy not happy? She tried to keep to herself so that she could figure out if she wanted to go any further with Alfred or not. Against her better judgment, Mercy decided not to see Alfred anymore. When he came to see her, she told him how she felt and let him know that this was too much for her right now. Alfred was very upset because he cared about Mercy. After the breakup with Alfred, Mercy found out that she was pregnant for a second time. Mercy was afraid and confused. "What am I going to do now?" thought Mercy. She felt like she couldn't tell anyone for fear of how they would think of her. Mercy knew that she wasn't financially ready or physically ready for another child. Mercy finally got up the courage to talk to the only person that she could think of in at a time like this: her mother. Mercy told her mom about her current situation and she asked Mercy if Alfred knew. Mercy said that she didn't want to complicate things any more by telling him. The next day Mercy called a clinic and made an appointment to have an abortion. The appointment was a week away. It seemed like an eternity to Mercy because she had to deal with the morning sickness and everything else all over again. Man, oh man, what rotten luck, thought Mercy. All she could do was cry because of the shame that she felt.

The day of the procedure finally arrived. Mercy was so nervous. She didn't know what to do or what to expect. She looked at David with tears in her eyes because she felt like she was disappointing him. Mercy picked her son up and began to rock him as she wept. She wiped her eyes, kissed him, and told him that she would be back later. William looked after him while she and her mother went to the clinic. Once there, Mercy began to shiver because it was so cold in the building. The receptionist had her to sign in and take a seat with the other women waiting to be called for their procedure. It was finally Mercy's turn. Once called, she had to put on a hospital gown. They took her to a room and she lay on a table. An IV was started, and not too long after that Mercy was out. When the procedure was finished Mercy was wheeled to a recovery room with the other women that had gone before her. Dazed and confused, Mercy felt very tired. All she wanted to do was sleep. They gave her juice and cookies afterward to give her energy so she could get ready to go home. This felt like one of the worst days of Mercy's life. Her mother allowed her to stay in her old room for the night so she could get some much-needed rest. The next day Mercy felt a whole lot better but continued thinking about what had taken place the day before. This was definitely an experience that she hoped to never have to go through again. Hopefully if there were to be any other relationships in the future she knew what and what not to do.

XIII

It Was Just a Part of His Plan

By now Mercy was well acquainted with people in the neighborhood. She got to know some of her mother's friends on a different level. One of these friends of her mother's asked Mercy if she would like to hang out with her one night, and Mercy didn't know why but she said yes. With no questions asked, Mercy's mom said she would watch David so that Mercy could go out. Mercy figured that since this was her mom's friend she should be okay. Janet came to Mercy's house to pick her up around nine in the evening. While riding, everyone in the car was drinking. Janet asked Mercy if she wanted some of the alcohol and Mercy said yes. Mercy remembered what happened to her awhile back with alcohol, so she drank a little this time and did not mix what she was drinking. Before she knew it they were in New York and pulling up to what looked like an abandoned parking lot with a small building in the middle of it. Mercy was afraid but couldn't do anything because she didn't know where she was, so she pretended like everything was okay. The man that drove them there knocked on the door of the building. Someone looked at him through a peephole and afterward opened the door. To her amazement, what looked abandoned on the outside didn't look bad on the inside. There were tables and a DJ playing music, and they even had food. "Wow," thought Mercy and began to get a little more comfortable. Once inside, they found a table. Not too long after that they were on the floor dancing and enjoying themselves.

The night seemed really nice. It seemed as though nobody left to go outside and no one new entered the club. Just when Mercy thought things couldn't get any more interesting, she was invited into the ladies room. In the ladies room were women smoking weed. And along with the weed they were putting their faces down on a piece of paper, and when they came back up they sniffed the air real hard. Because of the small crowd that had gathered in the bathroom, Mercy couldn't get a good look at what was really going on. Janet called Mercy over to her in the bathroom and introduced Mercy to some of the other women in the bathroom. Janet also had something in her hand in a dollar bill. It was a white powder that she bent down and sniffed really hard. After she finished, she passed it to another woman, who did the same thing. Janet told Mercy not to be afraid, just take a small amount. It would help her to have a little bit more fun and loosen her up some. Against everything that Mercy told herself, she bent down and sniffed the substance into her nostrils. The powder was strong and burned the inside of her nose. After this Mercy didn't really notice any difference in how she felt. She left the bathroom and went back over to where they were seated. Mercy waited to see if she could feel anything happening to her. Nothing as of yet, so she went and bought a drink. Before she knew it, Mercy was back on the floor enjoying herself and dancing up a storm. Janet and the others decided that it was time for them to leave. Mercy hated to leave but knew she had other responsibilities to get back to. Upon leaving the club, Mercy noticed that it was daybreak and the sun was shining bright outside. "Wow," thought Mercy, "how long were we in that club?" It was afternoon of the next day when they left. Mercy thanked Janet for showing her such a good time. Another experience, thought Mercy, but what was the point? She just didn't understand.

Mercy was now accustomed to drinking every now and then. She also smoked weed a little more often. Whenever she wanted to forget things at least for a little while, she would get high. Mercy kept it to only alcohol and weed; the cocaine wasn't her thing. One day she came home to a note slid under her door. Upon opening it she saw that it was from her neighbor's boyfriend. In the note he confessed to wanting to see her and not to tell his girlfriend. Mercy tore up the note. The next time she saw her neighbor she told her about the note. The very next time she saw John he began cussing her and choking her. It took everything that Mercy had in her that day to get him off of her. Mercy was now afraid to tell her neighbor for fear of what her boyfriend would do next. That was the last straw. Mercy now prepared to move. Not knowing where she would go next, Mercy called Leslie and let her know what happened. Being the friend that she was, Leslie asked her aunt if Mercy and David could stay with her for a while. Leslie's aunt let Mercy and David stay with her and her family. God showed up on her behalf again. Leslie's aunt didn't live too far from Mercy's mom. What difference did it make? It was as if Mercy's mom didn't even exist. As long as Mercy found somewhere to stay, and besides, with her things were good.

Chapter 13

MINISTRY MOMENT

Exodus 33:14, "God said, 'My presence will go with you. I'll see the journey to the end.'"

No matter how bad things seem to be, God is with you. If you let Him, He will begin to work in your life like never before. What we must realize is that we were placed here for His glory to shine through our lives. We should not be living defeated lives, because we belong to the great creator. If we took our minds off of everything that is wrong and placed our minds and our hearts on God, our lives would be so amazing.

Proverbs 3:5–6, "Trust in the Lord with all your heart and lean not to your own understanding. In all your ways acknowledge Him and He will direct your path."

Just know that if you're not living for God, then you're not really living.

A Closing Prayer

Father, I come to You in the Mighty Name of Jesus. I ask that you would touch everyone who reads this book. Let them see their need for You in their life. Let them know that they do matter and they do have a purpose in You. Touch their hearts and let them want to live for You. Let them see how important they are to You. Continue to bless them and show them your unconditional love. In Jesus's precious name I pray. Amen.

A Sinner's Prayer

Dear Lord, I am a sinner. I sinned against You and I sinned against heaven. Please come into my heart and make me a new creature. You said that if I confess with my mouth and believed in my heart, that Jesus died on the cross and on the third day He rose from the dead and is now seated at the right hand of the father, that I would be saved. Jesus, I now receive You as Lord and Savior of my life. Thank You, Lord, for saving my soul from eternal damnation. I promise to live my life for you. I can do all things through Christ, who strengthens me. In Jesus's name. Amen!

I could go on forever about how God has saved me. He has constantly kept His hands on me for such a time as this. The Bible tells us that our latter days shall be greater than our beginning. I used to wonder why. Not anymore, because I see that God has a purpose and a plan for my life. If you're reading this book, that means He has one for yours too. If you don't have one, get a relationship with Him. He will begin to show you how meaningful your life can be if you give yourself to Him. I never would have thought in a million years that I would be writing a book. It's not just any book, this is my story. God has taken someone like me and given me a story that will help heal someone else. That's what it's all about: reach one, teach one. If this book has helped you in any way with some of your life experiences, pray and ask God to help you so that in turn you can help someone else. I pray that this book has touched you in one way or another. If you haven't gone through anything like the story that is told in this book, then maybe you know someone who did. Seek God on how to reach out to someone who might be in need of a friend or maybe just a listening ear. Let God use you to show forth His love, and watch what you receive in return.

God bless you.